While every precaution has been taken in the preparation of this book, the publisher assumes no responsibility for errors or omissions, or for damages resulting from the use of the information contained herein.

BACK TO EDEN GARDENING: THE EASY ORGANIC WAY TO GROW FOOD

First edition. May 8, 2018.

Copyright © 2018 Bo Tucker.

ISBN: 978-1386196419

Written by Bo Tucker.

Back to Eden Gardening

The Easy Organic Way to Grow Food

Sign Up for Free Weekly Recipes, Tips and Tricks and more at:

http://www.FunHappyLives.com

Introduction

If you've ever seen the Back to Eden gardening film by Paul Gautschi, you'll find the easiest way to garden on earth. It details a garden system that requires minimal watering, minimal weeding, and minimal labor. The secret is that you need to keep a covering for your soil. It's organic gardening, also known as gardening God's way. It can transform your personal garden and provide a food solution that can work for your family and others.

The food your garden yields will be off the chats nutritionally, and it'll be fresh and pesticide free. Too many stores are carrying food that is water logged without the needed nutrients to keep you and your family sated and healthy. When you use the Back to Eden method, then this no longer is a problem. There is no reason that you should settle for overpriced food that isn't providing you with the nutrition that you need to stay healthy.

It also allows you to gain a level of independence from the intuitionally processed food that's rampant in America. In the film, Paul points out that the earth has covering to protect the soil from sun and erosion, but modern farming or even gardening methods remove that cover, leaving the soil bare. When a farmer tils the field, they're exposing the fungi in the soil to harmful ultraviolet rays. This will kill it and so will the wind. Most people who garden end up doing the same but on a smaller scale, which makes gardens require a large amount of water because the soil will dry too quickly. With the Back to Eden gardening method, anyone can grow food for themselves and their family with little to no work. All you have to do is garden the way that God intended.

Chapter 1: Comparing it to Other Methods

B efore you can get started with your Back to Eden gardening, you need to understand how it works in comparison to other gardening methods. Many people may swear by the gardening method they're currently using, but the Back to Eden method is proven to help you grow a sustainable garden that produces a high yield over time.

Conventional Gardening

Most people start with this gardening method. Even though it's not the best one out there. The main advantage of this type of gardening is that it's considered a cheap gardening style. You'd spread compost or manure on top and till it in to give your plants the nutrients you need, and you'd need to water by hand. Sadly, the bare soil means you'll need to deal with weeds and spend the time pulling them. This gardening doesn't have much of an upfront cost, but it does require labor if you want to maintain it.

Since the soil will compact and harden throughout the year without a cover, you will also need to use a till or spade to loosen it prior to planting. You will then need to make sure you don't compact the soil near the plants, meaning you'll need to stay out of your garden after you're done watering it. Tilling is one of the biggest drawbacks to this type of gardening, so either you spend hours doing it yourself or a lot of money on a rotor tiller if you want to do a larger scale garden. A rotor tiller will only loosen the soil about six inches down too, which your roots will go much deeper than that.

Using Raised Beds

———

If you didn't star twitch the traditional gardening method, you likely started with raised beds. These can quickly get expensive when you're first making them, but they can be maintained. Most people will fill them with growing soil from a nursery to start out with, but it's about forty dollars a yard. Even if you start hauling in manure, weeds are going to come with it. Though, since raised beds give you easy access to your garden, it will help you to keep the weeds under control.

Still, you have to pluck the weeds out by hand. The best part about raised gardening is that you can start with great soil without having to build the soil up, allowing you to plant what you want immediately. It will also allow for a higher yield at first, but the yield diminishes at the soil starts to dimension the following year. Another major problem, besides the cost of lumber, is the watering.

Watering by hand usually isn't practical, especially if you live in a dry climate. Setting it up where you have a watering system is yet another thing you'll need to pay for. You will also need to deal with soil compaction issues. In the first year you'll have freshly made soil that's loose, but as time goes on, you'll need to loosen the soil for planting. Still, the cost is the biggest drawback along with labor.

Back to Eden

Now that you know the flaws in two of the main gardening systems out there, you can rest assured that there is a better way. With he Back to Eden style, you'll be producing a higher yield I no time at all with little work through organic methods. You'll need four to six inches of organic covering, which usually is mulch. This will need to stay on your soil year round, and it will fix the issues that the other styles have. The sun will not hit your soil, which will keep it from killing the healthy microbes your plants need. Since you have mulch covering the soil, it will dramatically reduce the compaction, meaning you will not have a need to till the soil. This reduces the labor that will be needed to maintain your garden.

It'll also reduce the water evaporation which means you won't need to water your garden nearly as much. The mulch even cuts down on your weeding since it suppresses weed growth. The covering will eventually decompose, which in turn will fertilize your soil, so you can say goodbye to expensive fertilizers. It's also a cheap option for gardening, which means you'll have less startup cost up front. You can get many covering materials for free, such as the wood chips that are used in the Back to Eden documentary. With the Back to Eden method, it's even easier to access your garden during bad weather since it decreases the mud.

One of the biggest myths about the Back to Eden method is that the carbon rich material that is on top of your soil will rob the nitrogen from the soil when it decomposes. This simply isn't true. The top one-sixteenth of an inch of your soil is in contract of the covering, and that's all that will be affected. As long as your covering is laying on top of your soil instead of being mixed in, you will not have an issue.

Chapter 2: Getting the Right Covering

———

O nce you've decided to give the Back to Eden gardening method a try, you'll need to decide on the right covering for you. There are many different options that you can use with the Back to Eden method, but Paul uses woodchips in the film.

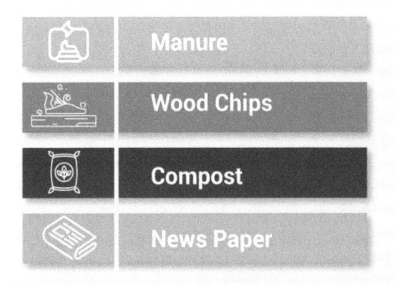

Layers

Using Wood Chips

In the Back to Eden film, wood chips were the covering of choice, and part of the reason is that you can often get them for free from tree trimming companies. However, if you can't go get them yourself, you may have to call around to see which companies are willing to deliver directly to your home. There are some tree trimming companies that even have a list that you can sign up for, but that can take several weeks or more. You don't have to limit your search to tree trimming companies either. Some people will even find wood chips from the electric company since they clear out places for power lines, and you can often get a hold of the foreman for the crew.

However, you're likely to get larger types of wood chips this way. In the Back to Eden film, you see small wood chips that are about an inch, but you can get wood chips that are up to eighteen inches long, and many of them will be four inches long if you aren't careful. Bigger wood chips will leave bigger gaps in your soil, so it makes for worse mulch. They also dry out quickly, which makes the decomposition slow. With free wood chips, you're likely to be dealing with more work.

The wood chips in the Back to Eden film were processed using a tub grinder. This grinds chips smaller than tree trimming companies. When you get the right wood chips, don't be surprised with how quickly they decompose. Even if you leave them in a pile, they're likely to decompose quickly. If kept moist, wood chips break down quickly. The easiest way to move wood chips around is using a pitchfork. It slices into your wood chip pile easier than a shovel, but don't expect moving wood chips to be an easy task.

You may also want to use a wheelbarrow, moving them from the stack with the pitchfork, into your wheelbarrow and then depositing them where you need them to be. Don't be discouraged at the amount of woodchips it'll take to cover your garden when you need it to be four to six inches deep either. Even wood chip piles that are about the size of a car will likely cover 350 square feet or less. You also need to check to see how deep you're covering is after the wood chips have settled. One of the most mind blowing aspects of wood chips, is that they are actually lighter than dirt. Still, a storm or wind will not blow them away like topsoil does. The covering will continue to do its job, just as you see in the Back to Eden film.

Sawdust

————

Sawdust is not covered in the Back to Eden film, but it is another type of covering that you can use. If you're having a hard time getting the right type of wood chips in your area, then consider sawdust as an alternative. There are many success stories out there about using sawdust, but you should avoid sawdust that had turpentine in it. So, try to avoid sawdust that is too fine. If it's too fine, then water will not penetrate it. If you're going for sawdust, aged sawdust is usually best.

You'll also want the type that's made from chainsaws since it is fine without being too fine. It'll hold moisture well, and it'll break down quickly into a compost. Many people have local sawmills around them, but they likely won't deliver it to you. Sadly, most of these places will charge you at least a little for the sawdust. You may only pay for five dollars a load though. Just shop around and see what you can find in your area. You may get lucky and find someone willing to give it to you for free!

Other Mulching Alternatives

———

You may be wondering about what other mulching alternatives you have. Some people wonder if they can use leaves, hay or even straw. These are acceptable coverings. A thick layer of straw will reduce your need for watering or weeding. Though, if straw isn't readily available to you, you'll want to substitute. If you buy hale bales, you can easily set up a composting system, which will turn them into a great cover for your garden. The problem with these materials is that you will hardly ever find them free, and the actual price will depend on their availability in your area.

If you want to try to get hay bales for free, put up an ad for spoiled hay. You may find people that are willing to give you the hay bales for free or cheap to get them off their property if they spilled. This will help you to save a little money while still finding a decent mulch for your garden. When you decide to garden with hay bales, you need to be careful to sort out the seeds in your bales. They can be riddled with weed seeds or grass seeds. This is why you don't want to apply them directly to your garden. You also need to be sure that the hay wasn't sprayed with herbicides, which can ruin your garden for years to come.

Herbicides will commonly survive composting, and they can remain in your soil for up to seven years. For the same reason, you may want to avoid using grass clippings as your mulch. Many grassy areas are sprayed with herbicides, so you can't just pick them up from a landscaping company. On the other hand, leaves do not carry the risk of contamination. If you can locate a quantity large enough, leaves become a decent mulch. You just need to wet them thoroughly after covering your soil with them. This will keep them from being blown away.

Another Note

———

No matter what type of covering you're using, you'll also want to use newspaper or cardboard. This will nearly eliminate your grass and weeds that grow up through your covering. Just like the Back to Eden method teaches you, you will not need to till your soil. If it's hard as rock, just don't plant right away. The soil will start to loosen as time goes by after you apply your covering. It's best to apply your covering in fall. If you do this, then you can usually plant by the following spring. Remember do not mix in your covering!

More about Woodchips

———

You already know that wood chip gardening really works, and it's usually the best covering for your Back to Eden garden. Though, you may want to know a little bit more about woodchips before you go searching for them for your garden. In the film Back to Eden, wood mulch is actually recommended.

Build It Up

———

You'll want to build up your mulch in layers to get the best results. You'll want to start with your finer mulch at the bottom, putting a medium grade on top, and you can put a coarse mulch on top of that. As your mulch begins to decompose, you'll naturally be building up these layers again. The finer mulch will bread down, and the other will start to as well. So as your fine mulch is absorbed, you have top layers to take its place. You don't have to layer it all at once, though. You can layer fine mulch one year, and the following year place your medium grade on. The next year, try to place your larger mulch on it.

Add in Manure

———

Even in the Back to Eden film, manure was used. They practically used chicken manure, but there are many options available depending on where you are. You shouldn't apply manure too often. You should only scatter manure on top about once a year to get everything going. Though, some people have success spreading it every six months.

Color Matters

––––––––

The color of your mulch can matter as well. If you have colder weather, dark mulch will actually grow heat. This is great for northern states, which will help to warm your soil more. However, a lighter mulch will keep your soil cool. If you're in southern states, try a light wood chip or shaving. The lighter mulch reflects some of the heat back off the soil. It can also help in conserving water because it doesn't dry out nearly as fast despite the heat.

Don't Go for Looks

———

Thin tree branches, preferably with leaves that are shredded and composted are best for your garden. However, most people seem to lean towards mulch made out of bark because it looks better. This is the worst type of mulch for your garden! If you're trying to plant trees or shrubs, you'll probably want to use fresh wood chips because they're easy to get ahold of. However, if you're trying to plant vegetables, then fresh wood chips aren't a great idea. Over time, they make great composted wood chips, but right away they do little to no good. If all you see is shredded wood, then it isn't good for your garden. If all you see is bark, then stay away from it.

Woodchip Myths

There are many woodchip myths out there, which have convinced people that woodchips are bad for their garden when this isn't the case. Woodchips are successfully used in the Back to Eden film, and they've been successfully used by many gardeners long before the film hit its popularity.

They'll Acidify Your Soil

———

There is no evidence that actually supports this myth. The pH maybe fluctuate in your lower layer where it's decomposing, but it hasn't been proven to negatively affect your actual soil. In the Back to Eden film, you'll hear Paul talk about how it was tested that the pH balance in a garden in Canada had acidic soil and was afraid that woodchips and pine needles would raise it further. However, when a heavily wooded area that was producing healthy trees was tested, there was virtually no difference despite the vast amount of decomposing material on the ground.

Your Soil Will be Robbed of Nitrogen

———

We've already briefly covered this myth, and we've decided that it isn't true because the covering is not actually being mixed in with your soil. Once again, this is why it's important that you do not mix your covering with your soil. When you properly apply your woodchips, you will not need to worry about this.

They Attract Termites

This is yet another myth. Woodchips do not attract termites. Termites are a part of nature, and it's their job to decompose limbs and stumps that people don't remove. These areas may be attractive to termites if they randomly find them, but they will not attract termites. Termites cannot smell mulch, so they will not go seeking your garden out.

It's a Fire Hazard

There are occasional reports at facilities hosting piles of wood chips where heat is generated by the biomass within the pile that result in a fire. Even if you leave your woodchips in a pile, it should not generate enough heat to cause a fire. If you are still uncomfortable because of this myth, then you can spread your chips out when you get them or at least break them up into smaller piles. However, smaller piles will result in less compost.

Cedar Chips Leach Chemicals

———

First, you need to realize that cedar chips actually are a natural insect repelling wood. There are very few species of woodchips that contain the chemicals that kill seedlings and other plants. That chemical is allopathic. The trees to avoid are red cedar, red maple, black walnuts, sour orange, box elder, mango and eucalyptus. Normal cedar does not do this.

Choosing a Location

While you can use the Back to Eden gardening method no matter where you are, you may still want to put some thought into your location if you want to save yourself some time. Your success, or how long it takes you to reach success, can depend on the thought you put into your location. If you have a lot that has choices, then choose carefully when given the chance.

Look at the Convenience

———

Your convenience is important when choosing your garden location. A vegetable garden is meant for you to enjoy it as well as yield vegetables that you can savor. If you have to walk quite a way to get to your garden, then the chances are you're less likely to want to maintain it. Luckily, the Back to Eden method doesn't require too much work, some labor will always be there. Also, you're likely to miss out on harvesting ripe vegetables until it's too late if you aren't visiting your garden often enough. Despite your labor being cut down with this method, you still have to harvest regularly.

Look at the Sunlight

———

You also need to think about how much sun the location gets because different plants will require different amounts of sunlight. Most vegetables need six hours of sun, but some vegetables do even better with eight hours. This should be a huge consideration when you're deciding where to put your garden. In most cases, your vegetables need to have the most sun they can get, which will allow them to grow quickly and healthily.

Think about Wind

———

High winds will wreak havoc on your garden, even when you use woodchips to cover it. Try to think about where the wind usually comes from on your property, and then look for a place that would provide at least a little protection from those winds.

Consider Drainage

———

Just like plants can get too little water, they can get too much too. Waterlogged soil will kill your plans, so you don't want to have it at the bottom of a drainage area. For example. If you have a hill on your property, then you don't want to put your garden at the bottom. When it rains, your garden will have a hard time drying. This will cause your plants to suffer and possibly even die.

Soil Deserves Some Attention

Though with the Back to Eden gardening method your soil isn't as important as with traditional methods, you may still decide to give it a little attention when picking a location. If you have several locations, then you may want to consider the soil. If you have only one or two, then you don't need to think too much about it. The only thing you'd want to avoid is if rocks are in your soil.

Ease of Watering

———

When using the Back to Eden gardening method, you don't have to water nearly as much, watering is still going to be necessary on occasion. At a bare minimum, you'll need to water right after the initial planting. In the film, there is no watering required during the summer, but some people have a hard time making this work in their own climates. Don't be afraid to water occasionally, but remember that you don't need to do it all the time. Some people do have to water about ten times during the summer months, and this means you'll want to put your garden near a water source to make it easier.

More for Your Garden

———

When you've decided where you want your garden, there are still a few things that you'll need.

Get a Weed Barrier

———

A weed barrier to your soil will decrease the amount of weeds you're going to have to deal with. This is especially important in your first year, since the first year is usually the worst. However, make sure that you get a biodegradable weed barrier. That's where newspaper and cardboard usually come in handy. A single layer of cardboard will do the trick, or you can use four layers of newspaper to work as well. Some people want to double that amount of newspaper for the best results, depending on your location. It can be easy to acquire cardboard boxes.

Just check your local businesses and stores. There may even be a cardboard recycling center near you. Local newspaper companies will usually offer you old newspaper or unsold ones at a discounted price if not free as well. There are other biodegradable weed barriers you can buy, but usually they aren't worth the price. It's best to but down a little at a time, and make sure that you apply your weed barrier when there's no wind so that it doesn't get blown around while you're trying to work on your garden.

Consider Compost

If your soil is already great for growing, then you may not need it. However, applying several inches of compost over the soils recommended for most people. If you're buying bagged compost, it's likely going to get expensive. This is why composted manure is so popular, and it's shown in the Back to Eden film. You can usually find this for free, and it doesn't' take too much searching. A horse can produce fifty pounds of manure each day, and usually the owner is more than happy to get rid of. However, cow manure usually has fewer weeds to worry about. If you live around people that have livestock, you may be lucky enough to find people with piles that have aged more than a year. Spread it over your weed barrier, several inches thick, so that it provides nutrients for at least a few years for your plant.

Think about Settling

———

You already know that your next step with the Back to Eden gardening style is putting down your cover. No matter what cover you choose, it's going to be tricky to get the right depth. Yes, in theory you want four to six inches. After six inches, it can be hard to move it aside to plant. Though, you want that depth after everything has settled for several weeks. With woodchips in particular, settling can be a big deal. You may apply eight inches of wood chips, and it can settle to about five inches in less than a week. If you have wood chips that are coarser, you're going to want to lean towards a thicker covering because chunky woodchips allows for air to pass between them. In turn, this allows needed moisture to escape. The best plan of action is to start with a minimum of covering, and layer on as necessary so that it isn't too light or too thick.

When You Start Planting

———

P lanting is considered the fun part in gardening, and once you have mimicked nature in your garden, then you're able to get started. When using the Back to Eden method, the planting is similar to any gardening method. The difference is that you will be moving the covering to plant your seeds.

Using Stakes

———

I t can be easy to use two metal stakes that are connected by a piece of twine, arranging your rows with it. Place your stakes a part at both ends, and then pound the stakes into your ground. Rack the covering back so that your soil is exposed. You can then move the stakes over three to four feet, repeating the process. This will give you straight rows to work with, and then you can go back and plant in the exposed soil.

Using Transplants vs Seeds

———

I f you've decided to transplant instead of using seeds, you'll need to cover them back up around the stem. If you are going to use seeds instead, you'll want to leave the soil bare for a bit. Seeds don't do well growing through even a little covering. In a few weeks, you'll need to come back and spread the covering, but this is only after your seeds are a few inches tall. One thing to watch out for is that you want to have the covering far enough away from your rows that they won't slide and smother a plant that's trying to sprout. This can be a problem, especially if you're dealing with wind.

The Exception

———

If you're growing potatoes, you won't have to worry about them being covered. They'll grow through a foot of woodchips, so you can cover them back with your covering immediately and not have to worry about them. This makes potatoes a great plant to start with. Like with any Back to Eden grown vegetable, you'll get a high yield.

The Spacing

———

The spacing is about the same with Back to Eden gardening as it is with a conventional garden. However, over time you're likely to need to increase the space. Your soil will be loose and fluffy, meaning the root systems of your plant will grow larger then they normally do. This results in large plants with a high yield. In the Back to Eden film, Paul talks about how his trees require twice the recommended spacing, but that's because they grow double the side and produce more too.

Your Watering & Fertilizing Needs

―――――

With a thick layer of mulch, your watering needs are drastically reduced. In the film, you'll see that Paul doesn't have any watering problems. Sadly, this doesn't work for everyone with the Back to Eden method because people live in different clients. Your water needs will be reduced to a fraction of what they used to be. The most critical time for your plants to get the water they need is when they're still planting.

Since you can't cover them up immediately without smothering them, you'll want to take care of the soil and keep it moist the old fashion way. Your watering will start to go down significantly as the roots start to develop. After the first few weeks, you can cut your watering down to every other week or every three weeks. Of course, it's better to watch your plants and judge based on the climate how much to water your plants. The quality of covering you're using will matter too.

Fertilizing Your Garden

———

S ome people get upset when it come stop the Back to Eden style because they have a hard time getting the large, healthy plants that they saw in the film. If you're a first time gardener, you're going to make some mistakes. Good soil doesn't happen overnight, and you can't just throw down the covering and walk away and expect great yield. Some people even think that fertilizer isn't required because the covering would decompose. This is true over time, but this can take years. Only one to two inches of your covering will decompose a year.

This means that only a quarter inch of compost will be created every year. The soil becomes richer as the years go by. Not weeks. You'll want to apply fertilizer before your covering is applied. When applying it, you need to apply enough for several years. After about a decade, you'll have fantastic soil, but you'll need to make due until then. As your covering thins out, you'll be adding more. This means you'll eventually reach the level of richness that Paul has in the film. If you've messed up and already applied your covering, your compost can still be applied. The rain will eventually wash it down into the soil, but it will cause your covering to decompose faster. The downside is that wees will grow from the manure if it isn't covered.

Weeds are Inevitable

———

Some weeds are simply inevitable even if you use the Back to Eden gardening method. While the amount may be cut down, you need to learn to handle weeds effectively and organically. Depending on your location will depend on what type of weed you're dealing with. Since your soil is loose instead of compact, it'll be easy to weed your garden when you do have to. In this chapter, we'll cover some organic weeding tips to make your life a little easier.

Use the Crowding Method

———

It's easier to crowd your vegetables when your roots are growing out more, but when you're just getting started, it can be difficult. Mulching will cut down on some weeds by smothering them, but crowding can help you to get rid of the rest. If there's no space for weeds, then they can't take over your garden. It's okay if your plants touch during their maturity. The leaves that grow between the rows will deprive weeds of sunlight, keeping them from taking up.

Limited Tilling

―――

This is a natural weeding method of the Back to Eden gardening method. Since you don't need to till and dig all the time, you aren't bringing new weed seeds to the surface of your garden. When you are planting your seedlings for the first time, don't dig further than you need to so that you don't pull up anything unnecessarily.

Use Boiling Water

This can be difficult to do for a large garden, but if you're just getting started this can be an easy method. It's great if you're dealing with a particularly stubborn patch. If you pour boiling water over your weeds, it'll burn them. When the water cools, it'll run down into the soil to keep it damp to. Just make sure that you don't pour boiling water over your plants, or you'll kill them too.

Use Vinegar

Vinegar is a great household remedy for weeds, and it's a completely organic method that goes great with the Back to Eden method. Use a gallon of 5% white vinegar, then add in a cup of table salt and tablespoon of dish soap. You'll want to mix everything together, and then put it in a spray bottle. Spray it directly onto your weeds. Just like with boiling water, you'll want to avoid spraying it on your plants. This method works best if you're doing it during the day when the sun is shining. However, if you want to get twenty or thirty percent vinegar, it'll be even stronger. The vinegar is too acidic at that point to handle without goggles and gloves though, so most people prefer to use household vinegar.

Use Corn Gluten

———

This is a byproduct of corn milling, and it'll keep feed seeds from germinating in your garden. However, you cannot use this method when you are trying to sprout your seeds or it will kill them too. It's a non-toxic and organic material, and most people can find it in their local garden center. If all else fails, you should be able to find it online.

Owning Chickens & Weeds

In the Back to Eden film, Paul did have chickens, and he used them in his gardening. Everything has a purpose, and if your weeds sprout, you can actually feed your chickens the weeds! This is a great use of them, and they'll seem like less of a nuisance if your chickens are getting something out of them. When your chickens eat the weeds, you can think of it as it going towards your manure. It's free chicken food. If you have waste in your garden, then you may want to feed it to your chickens too. Damaged vegetables can be given to your chickens, and they'll give you eggs in return.

More Reasons to Get Chickens

I n the Back to Eden film, Paul's chickens are not free range, but the choice is still yours. There are many benefits to both free-range chickens and those kept in a coop. Paul keeps his chickens in a coop and run, which also doubles as his compost! Here are some more reasons to keep chickens around, no matter what you decide.

Eggs

Eggs are an obvious reason to keep chickens around. There are various reasons that your own eggs from your own birds are better, and one of those reasons is that it's full of nutrients. You know that the chickens laying your eggs are healthy, and you don't have to worry about getting them sick nearly as much as people think. You can also raise different breeds to get different colored eggs. The quality of your egg goes up, and they're free!

GMO Free

———

You know that your food is GMO free when you get your eggs yourself, especially if you are using leftovers from your garden and organic chicken feed. What your animals eat will also depend on the quality of eggs you get. Even the meat is more nutrient dense when you raise your own chickens.

Small Amounts of Space

———

C hickens don't take up that much room. They're great even if your Back to Eden garden is in your backyard. All you need is a coop and a small run, but if you have more space you can create a bigger flock.

Self-Sufficiency

Many people choose to get chickens for the same reason that people start a Back to Eden garden. By raising chickens, you're choosing a level of self-sufficiency. You can raise your won meat and your own eggs, providing you and your family with the protein that you need.

Compost

J ust like with Paul in the Back to Eden garden, your chicken waste is a great compost, or the coop can be your compost heap all in itself. Nutrient rich soil is a must for a Back to Eden garden, and chicken waste is a great organic matter to use.

It's Affordable

R aising your own chickens are also affordable. You don't need much initial startup. You'll need next to none if you're deciding on free range chickens. Otherwise, you'll need to build a chicken coop and run, which also means getting chicken wire. Once everything is set up, you're much less likely to have reoccurring costs. You even cut down on garbage costs by feeding leftovers to them.

Weed Control

C hickens can become your perfect sidekick if you let them free range. They're a source of organic and free pest control. So you won't have to worry about those invasive weeds popping up everywhere. Give it one year and you'll be surprised just how tidy and neat your garden is.

Saving Heritage Birds

———

Today's chickens are not like their ancestors. Only certain chickens are good for meat, and others are bred simply for maximum egg production. You can add a rare heritage breed to your yard if you're just looking for eggs, which will help to save these birds.

Consider Ducks Instead

———

While chickens are featured in the Back to Eden film and are considered more traditional homesteading animals, here are a few reasons why you might want to consider gardening with ducks instead. You can use their droppings as manure too!

They're Quiet

C hickens are loud, and unless you have a big property you may not want to deal with that. Roosters aren't allowed in urban areas most of the time even if hens are. However, male ducks, which are called drakes, wont' even quack. They just make a raspy, soft sound. Female ducks will also lay their eggs quickly right before sunrise. They see no reason to let you know like chickens. You can easily keep a few females and even a drake in a backyard without more than the occasional quack. Ducks chatter quietly until they're excited or scared.

They're Gentle on Land

———

Ducks will nibble on your flowers and bushes, and they may even trample your lawn. However, they won't till your soil. If you want to go with free range, this makes ducks better than chickens for a Back to Eden garden. Chickens can scratch out your plant roots and make deep depression in your soil because they like to take dust baths. However, ducks will each ground cover so be weary! They still help with insect control and grub control too.

You Can Contain Them

———

Ducks are easier to contain than chickens. If you choose a domestic duck that can't fly, then it's easy to keep them in your backyard. Just don't choose Mallards. A two foot fence is usually enough to keep them confined. Comparatively, your chickens could clear a four foot fence. Though, ducks are vulnerable to injury or death from daytime predators such as hawks and dogs. It's best to keep them in an enclosed pen for their own safety if you aren't home.

They're Less Demanding

———

Ducks don't require as much for their housing. They don't need roosts or nesting boxes. You can use a small dog house, garden shed, tool shed or playhouse and turn it into a functional home for your ducks. All you need to do is attach a predator proof latch and make sure that some ventilation windows are included.

Ducks are Hardy

———

You can hardly find vets that are willing to treat livestock, so having ducks which are hardier comes in handy. They have a stronger immune system than chickens. Their normal temperature is about 107 degrees, making them resistant to bacteria and parasites. They aren't even acceptable to coccidiosis which chickens are. They also don't usually get sick from the avian flu even if they can still be carriers. Chickens will usually die from the avian flu if they come down with it. They also are less susceptible to mites, lice or other external parasites since they spend quite a bit of time in water.

Duck Eggs are Superior

―――

D uck eggs actually have more nutrition than chicken eggs. Duck eggs are richer in flavor and higher in fat. They're even better for baking. If you were going to buy duck eggs, they're actually more expensive too.

Chicken Composting

You'll see chicken composting in the Back to Eden film. The first thing you need to realize is that it's best to have a coop if you want to use this method properly. While free range chickens may sound nice, it can be more hassle than it's worth. It can be sad to keep chickens cooped up all the time, but finding your chickens dead because of predators can be just as sad if not more. You'll need to balance free time and keeping them safe, and with a coop you don't have to worry about finding the eggs.

Throw it In!

———

You'll want to throw compostable items into your coop. this includes when you prune your trees. Throw in the pruned branches into your chicken run. Only pull the branches out when all of the leaves have fallen off. You can then use your limbs for whatever you like. The leaves will be turned into compost by your chickens. The mother hen as well as her chicks tear at the leaves and you garden waste when you drop it into the run.

Make a Sifter

———

You'll need a compost sifter to use this method. You can use a piece of hardware cloth over a bucket or you can use a professional one. That's completely up to you and how much work you want to put into it. By sifting, you're keeping big pieces like rocks out of your garden. The only time that this step will not be necessary is if you are using the compost for fruit trees. If you're growing fruit trees, then you can shovel it into the wheelbarrow and move on to the next step immediately. While you may take the actual sticks out of the chicken run, there's no reason to take the twigs out. Everything will break down eventually. With time, they'll eventually turn to compost too.

Building a Sifter

———

You can even build a sifter for your wheel barrel, which will help if you are creating a large garden. To do this, you'll need to measure your wheelbarrow and make a frame that's big enough to go over it. You'll sandwich the hardware cloth in between the pieces of wood or staple it down to the frame. Next, just place the screen over your wheel barrel, and shovel the compost on top. Shake your screen, and he coarse material will be all that remains on top. You can discard the coarse material by placing it back on the ground. Repeat this process until your wheel barrel is full. You'll then want to tea a rake and rake your compost over existing soil.

Some FAQ

This is an easy FAQ for both the Back to Eden gardening method as well as some questions you may have about the Back to Eden film.

Why doesn't Paul raise his own chickens?

―――

It's simply easier for Paul to get twenty or so chicks every year or two than having to deal with hatching chicks. Without the hassle of hatching chicks, he is able to eat the eggs as well without any added complications.

What are his chickens fed?

―――

While you can feed chickens chicken feed, Paul feeds his chicken's table and garden scraps. If he has any leftover meat, then it goes to the dogs. This way nothing goes to waste with his Back to Eden gardening example. Paul prefers not to feed his chicken's chicken feed. However, he does have a trash can full of chicken feed in the chicken coop. he only plans to use this if it snows enough to stop the chickens from digging in the ground. If you want to keep an emergency bit of chicken feed for your chickens, don't worry about the brand. Just make sure that it's organic.

What about watering your chickens?

———

L ike any animal, chickens do need water. You may have missed the watering system he had for his chickens. It was simple, and you can see it in the first few seconds of the film. You'll see a shallow pan of water, which is what his chickens drink out of. He changes the water a few times a day. In the winter he has to replace frozen water just as often, especially if it's freezing out.

What about feeding chickens during winter?

———

If you want an easy crop to grow to feed your chickens during winter, then it's best to try to have Kale growing in your garden.

Do you have to worry about GMO seeds?

———

N o, it costs them too much money to sell or buy GMO seeds to an individual because of all of the contract involved. You would definitely know if you are buying GMO seeds, so you don't have to worry about the brand too much.

What if you only have indirect sunlight?

———

You can grow greens and root crops well even if you don't have direct sunlight. You might want to consider growing lettuce, spinach, kale, celery, cilantro, collards, parsley, onions, mustard greens, cauliflower, cabbage, broccoli, celery, beets, radishes, carrots and Brussel sprouts.

What if you live in an apartment?

———

Though the Back to Eden gardening method isn't meant to be used in this way, there's no reason you can't use the mulching method in potted plants. You should make the best of what you have, but the pots will keep your plants from growing nearly as large as they would be in an open plot. You won't get all the benefits from the Back to Eden method if you're using containers, and you'll need to water your plants more often.

What if I already tilled the area?

There's no getting around that this is bad news for your garden. When you tilled your soil you brought all of your good soil right to the top, and so everything that good is on the soil is now exposed to die. You also just pushed the bad soil down to where you'll be planting your seeds. You also just compacted the soil, and you'll need to work to get the soil better again.

Do you need to let the area rest?

If your ground isn't stressed, then there's no need to let the ground rest. In the film, Paul plants his crops in the same spot, and he doesn't see a need to rotate his crops on purpose.

Can you use this method for raised beds and containers?

———

Yes, you can but it does defeat the purpose of the Back to Eden method for many people. The only benefits you'll get is that you'll need to weed, fertilize and water more. The biggest issue you'll face with raised beds or containers is that four to six inches of loose covering can easily fall out if you don't have tall enough containers. Raised beds, like container, usually just don't have enough room.

Is the Back to Eden method good for the whole counter?

—————

It's not feasible at this time, but in time, then yes it would be. There are trees that grow every year, and people are cutting down trees every year as well. When you put your woodchips down, you'll be good for a while. You may only need to put them own twice, but you're welcome to do it more than that. If you have the right area with willing tree services, it won't be hard to do a few hundred acres. Though, with most places it'll be difficult to get the woodchips you'll need. You'll want to start with a smaller area and expand from there.

Will animal droppings and urine kill my garden?

———

U rine does have nitrogen, and your plants love nitrogen. However, if too much of anything, especially nitrogen, is put into one spot, it can have adverse effects on your garden. If your dog pees in the same spot again and again, then the spot will burn. This is due to over fertilization. Dogs and cats especially have a high nitrogen level in their waste because they eat protein. Chicken, cows, rabbits, sheep, goats and horses eat greens, so they have less nitrogen that you have to worry about. Still, it's best to let the waste from these animals sit before using them. You do not want to use waste from a dog or a cat. You need to keep your animals from going in the same spot each and every time either way.

How do you keep animals out of your garden?

———

It's best to use a dog if you're dealing with cougars or deer. You do not want your dog to become dinner for a bear, but it will tell you if there is a bear out there. If you don't have a dog, then try motion sensor sprinklers, which will turn the water on when you walk buy. You can also put up a fence, and you can hang pebbles and cans on the bigger plants. Some fine fishing line can help as well. There are some animals that are smarter than this, but if a deer walks into fishing line, they'll become confused and back up. In the Back to Eden film, Paul doesn't worry too much about animals eating the food until his dogs can drive them off.

Do pests serve any purpose?

———

Yes, there is a purpose in slugs, snails or other pests in your garden. If you want to get rid of them, then just use some natural pest control methods. However, this is not in the original Back to Eden garden model. Slugs with attack dying, stressed or dead plants. Every critter servers a purpose, so just look up the pest you have to see what may be wrong with your garden.

Will my trees sag down like in the film?

———

I n the film, Paul does not work to get his trees to sag down the way they are. It's because his ground is fertile enough to have the fruit start growing before the saplings can properly hold their weight. Two year old trees sometimes even need to be propped up with sticks because they have too many apples. Trees will sag naturally over time if you have fertile ground and good growing conditions.

A Little about Destructive Insects

—

E ven with the Back to Eden gardening method, you'll have a hard time keeping pests out. Over time it'll become easier, but here are some pests to worry about.

Slugs

———

This is one of the top horrors for many gardeners, especially if they're using a mulching method. If you have chickens, it's less likely that you're going to have an issue with slugs. Ducks and garter snakes can help too. Eggshell barriers sprinkled around your plants can help too, but it doesn't always work. Beer traps are a great way to get rid of slugs too. Feeding the slugs to your chickens will help them to produce eggs too!

Squash Bugs

If you're growing squash, this can be a huge worry. It doesn't matter if you're growing winter or summer squash because even ducks won't be able to help you. Handpicking is the best defense with this type of bug. If you clean up infested plants at the end of yours reason, it'll help to interrupt their life cycle. Spraying nee on egg clusters can help too if you're dealing with juvenile squash bugs. You can also use row covers, but this isn't used in most Back to Eden models. Some people even put open pizza boxes beneath your plants during a cool morning. Jostle your plant, and then the juvenile and adult squash bugs will fall off. Then slide the box out and then put them in a pail of soapy water.

Aphids

———

This is a common issue for anyone with an organic garden. If you want to get rid of these pear shaped bugs, then you will want to use water. A nice strong spray of water will help rinse them off the plants. However, you may also want to introduce native predators like aphid midges, lady beetles and lacewings. You can also see hot pepper or garlic repellent sprays. Horticultural oil can help too, but this is a more expensive option.

Scales

The adult females look like soft bumps that are on the stems, fruit or leaves. Males are small flying insects. The larvae are small and they have threadlike mouthparts. They can be found on indoor plants, ornamental shrubs, trees and fruit throughout North America. They suck the plant sap, which will weaken your plants. Your plants will start to yellow and their leaves may drop. Prune your infested plant to get rid of them, but soapy water can rinse them away too.

Cabbage Maggot

You're only going to have these issues if you are growing any cabbage family crops. The maggots aren't on the leaves either. They actually burrow into the roots, and they kill the plants that way. If they don't immediately kill your plants, they can leave entryways for diseases to take root. Floating row covers are the best organic method to take care of these pests.

Caterpillars

———

Caterpillars are a danger that every gardener knows about. They're larvae that chew on leaves or along margins. They tunnel into fruits to, so they won't just attack vegetables either. Hand picking them is easiest, but with some caterpillars this isn't an option. Remember that some can be poisonous to the touch.

Cutworms

———

These works can completely wreck your garden, and they're mainly active at night making them hard to see. They'll be found on early vegetables and flower seedlings. They can chew through the stems near the ground, and they're worse in May and June. Transplants or cutworm collars are best you may also want to delay planting, and you can look for them below the soil surface if you want to hand pick them.

Tarnished Plant Bug

―――――

These are fast moving bugs that can be mottled, brown or green. They also have black tipped yellow triangles on their wings. They're attracted to flowers vegetables and fruits. They suck plant juices in their nymph and adult stages. This causes the leaf and fruit to distort, stung grow, tip die back and it can cause wilting. If you keep your garden weed free, then you're less likely to deal with these bugs, which is an advantage of the Back to Eden method.

Potato Beetle

———

Also known as the Colorado potato beetle, they don't just stick to Colorado. They also eat potatoes, cherry tomatoes, egg plants, tomatoes and even petunias. They'll reduce the yield of your plant if not killing theme entirely. Straw mulches are a great way to rid of these bugs, so you're less likely to deal with them in the Back to Eden method.

Japanese Beetles

The adult Japanese beetle is a metallic blue green, and their larva is white with brown grubs. You'll find them east of the Mississippi River, and they'll eat leaves, chew flowers, and defoliate plants. The larvae feed on your garden roots and lawn. Shake beetles from the plants early in the morning.

Flea Beetle

―――

These are small dark beetles, and they'll eat through most crops in North America. They're more of a danger to vegetables than they are to fruit. They'll leave holes in your leaves, but they'll be relatively small. Either way, they can be especially damaging to large plants and the larvae will actually eat the plant roots. Garlic spray will usually take care of them.

Mexican Bean Beetle

These beetles look like a yellow version of the lady bug to many. They can be found in most states that are east of the Mississippi River, and you'll also find them in parts of Utah, Texas, Arizona, Nebraska, and Colorado. They'll chew on the leaves from beneath them, and they'll leave a lacy appearance. You can plant a soybean trap crop to get rid of them, and you can drawer their natural predator such as the spined soldier bug to your yard.

Insects That Are Good For Your Garden

———

Some insects are good for your garden, and God put them there for a reason. That's why you'll want to take a look at the bugs you want to keep around your garden even if you don't work to introduce them yourself.

Aphid Midge

———

Aphids wreck a garden, and this is an easy way to combat them. They feed on over sixty species of aphids, and they paralyze them with toxic salvia.

Barconid Wasps

The adult female is really the one you want around, but you need to take them all if you want their benefits. They infect their eggs into the host insect, which is usually beetle larvae, aphids, moths or caterpillars. They then feed on the host after the larvae hatch. The host dies when the larvae complete development, and they grow grown near dill, parsley, wild carrot, small flowers, nectar plants, and yarrow best.

Ground Beetles

———

Ground beets are great to get rid of cutworms, cabbage maggots, snails and even slugs. Those aren't the only pests they can help to get rid of either. A single beetle larva can eat more than fifty caterpillars, helping you do get rid of them. If you want to introduce a stable habitat for them, then include perennials. White clovers are also a great way to build ground beetles a habitat.

Lady Beetles

———

The adult lady beetle with eat mealybugs, mites and aphids. They larvae help even more too! If you want to attract them naturally to your garden, then plant yarrow, fennel, dill, angelica or even coreopsis.

Damsel Bugs

These feed on small caterpillars thrip, leafhoppers and aphids. You can collect them from an alfalfa field, sweet nest or just plant some alfalfa yourself!

Lacewings

———

B oth the larvae and adults are great for getting rid of caterpillars, thrips, scales, mealybugs, and whiteflies. You can grow sweet alyssum, angelica, cosmos or coreopsis if you want to attract them.

Minute Pirate Bugs

———

These are quick moving bugs that are primarily black and white. They'll attack almost any insect, so if you're having a big problem, then try to plant something that will form a natural habitat for them. Your best choices are goldenrods, alfalfa, yarrow, and daises.

Soldier Beetles

———

These soldier beetles can be soldiers for your natural pest control. They feed on caterpillars and aphids, but they don't stop there. They will also feed on beneficial species or just harmless ones, so you need to introduce them only if you really neeed them. If you want to attract them, plant hydrangea, goldenrod or catnip.

Tachinid Flies

The larva burrow into caterpillars, which will destroy them from the inside out. To attract them plant herbs like parsley or dill or even sweet clover.

Spined Soldier Bug

———

The spined soldier bug has pointed shoulders, and will distinguish them from the stink bug. If you want to attract them then make permanent beds of perennials. They'll provide shelter to them, and they'll even help with beetle larvae.

Hover Flies

These are bugs that remind you of bees, and they're a great natural predator to those that endanger your garden. The flies will look like bees or yellow jackets, but you'll notice they have two wings instead of four. Just plant plants that are rich in nectar and pollen to attract them. Two great plants to start with are buckwheat or mustard, which also are great to bring to your table. The larvae will attack bugs like mealybugs and aphids. A single hover fly larvae can eat over 400 aphids before they reach adulthood.

Assassin Bugs

———

You shouldn't let the name intimidate you with these bugs. They're natural predators to thrips, spiders, caterpillars and mites. They'll also help with other plant eating insects. Adults are usually brown or black with flat bodies. You'll want to include shrubs and bunch grass in your Back to Eden garden I you want to attract these.

Organic Pesticide Recipes

N ow that you know some of the most common pests to look out
for, you may wonder what organic pesticides you can buy or
make to take care of them. That's what this chapter is all about.

Neem Oil Spray

———

Ancient Indians used neem, and it's not hard to get neem oil. It's an all-natural plant that words off pests, and it's one of the most natural pesticide on the planet. It holds about fifty natural insecticides, and you can grow your own if you're up for it. To make your own neem oil spray, use the recipe below.

- ½ Once Neem Oil, High Quality
- ½ Teaspoon Liquid Soap, Organic
- 2 Quarts Water, Warm

Mix it all together, and then use a spray bottle. Shake well before each use.

Vegetable Oil Spray

———

A lso known as a white oils pray, you only need two ingredients. Soap and oil. Just make sure that you're using an organic soap. It'll repel aphids, mites and other soft body insects.

- 1 Cup Organic Liquid Soap
- 1 Cup Vegetable Oil

The soap allows the oil to stick to the bugs, so just mix a cup of oil with a cup of organic soap. Shake well, making it turn white, and dilute it before using it. Mix a tablespoon of this mixture to four cups of water. Reapply this to your plants every week. The concentrate will keep for about three months if you seal it in a mason jar.

Simple Salt Spray

―――

S alt is a great way to kill a lot of insects, especially slugs or snails. However, it won't do much for bugs like potato beetles or aphids.

- 2 Tablespoons Himalayan Crystal Salt
- 1 Gallon Water

Mix it all together, and then just spray the infected area.

Mineral Oil Spray

You're going to need a high grade mineral oil if you want this natural insectside to work. It works by dehydrating insects as well as their eggs.

- 25 ml High Grade Mineral Oil
- 1 Liter of Water

Mix together, and then add it to a spray bottle.

Cayenne Pepper & Citrus Spray

———

This is best on ants, which can be more of a pain than they're worth in your garden.

- 10 Drops Citrus Essential Oil
- 1 Teaspoon Cayenne Pepper, Ground
- 1 Cup Water, Warm

Mix it all together in a spray bottle, and shake well before each use.

Garlic Spray

Garlic is an antiviral, antibacterial and it has anti-fungal properties. This also makes it a potent pesticide. The best part is that it's cost effective with just a little work.

- 5-7 Bulbs Garlic
- 17 Ounces of Water

Just peel your garlic cloves and crush them. You should do about five to seven bulbs, and then mix your garlic with seventeen ounces of water. Let it sit for at least six hours, but longer is better. It works even better if you add in a dash of organic dish soap, and then pass it through a fine strainer. Dilute the mixture with a gallon of water, and then spray your plants once or even twice a week. You'll need to mix a new batch each week if you still want it to be potent. However, don't use this too close to your harvest because it can affect the flavor of your food. Also, a garlic spray will kill all insects that it comes into contact with, so it can destroy beneficial bugs too. You should only spray parts of the plants that are infested.

Epsom Salt Spray

E psom salt isn't just for your sore muscles. It can be used in your garden as well. You can sprinkle it around your plants if your problem is localized, but if you need to use a lot of it, it's best to use a spray.

- 1 Cup Epsom Salts
- 5 Gallons Water

Dissolve a cup of Epsom salt in five gallons of water, and then place some in a spray bottle. It'll work against slugs as well as beetles. Otherwise, you can simply sprinkle it around the base of your plants, replacing it every other week. It'll deter pests and increase the nutrition absorption of your plant roots. However, this is expensive and doesn't work as well with the Back to Eden method because you have mulch covering your roots.

Lemon Spray

———

C itrus will help with aphids, which are a plague on many peoples' gardens. All you need to do is grate the rind from a lemon to get started.

- Zest of 1 Lemon
- 2 Cups Water

Just place your lemon rind into the water and then boil it. Take it off of heat, and then allow the lemon rind to steep overnight. Strain the liquid using either a mesh sieve or a cheesecloth. Pour the liquid into a spray bottle, and then apply it to the top and underside of the leaves on your affected plant. This will only be effective if you spray it directly on the insects. If it does not come into contact with the bodies of the insects, it will not work.

Pepper Spray

M ost everyone knows how irritating hot peppers can be if they've touched their eyes or nose after cutting hot peppers. That's what makes it such an effective pesticide. Most gardening stores will already have natural hot pepper sprays available, but they can get pricy quickly. You can actually make your own at home. You'll need to start by wearing gloves though!

- 2 Cups Hot Peppers, Chopped (Habanero works great!)
- 1 Tablespoon cayenne Pepper
- 1 Bulb Garlic, Cloves Extracted & Peeled
- 4 Gallons Water
- 3 Tablespoons Organic Dish Soap

Start by preparing all of your ingredients, and then place your cayenne pepper, hot peppers and garlic in a food processor. Process until smooth, and then place the mixture in your four gallons of water. Let it steep for twenty-four hours, and then strain it. After straining, mix your dish soap in well, and pour some in a spray bottle. Apply liberally on your plants one to two times a week.

All Purpose Spray

———

This is an essential oil spray, and essential oils are great to use on your garden as well as all natural!

- 1 Teaspoon Vodka
- 10 Drops Lemon Essential Oil
- 10 Drops Cedar wood Oil
- 1 Ounce Water
- 10 Drops Eucalyptus Oil

Mix all ingredients together and place them in a glass spray bottle. Shake before each use.

Cedar Oil

———

C edar oil works best on visible insects and scale insects, and it kills them by drying out their outer shells. It can drive off any survivors because it has an irritating effect on their body. You'd need to spray the oil directly on visible pests, but you should be aware that it'll send gnats into flight. There are usually gnats around, but they stay hidden if they aren't irritated.

Just be careful because despite the great smell, it can still irritate your eyes and skin. Cedar oil is hard to get off of your skin too, so wearing gloves is best. You also shouldn't spray cedar oil into the wind since it can irritate your nasal passages and eyes. When you go to spray it on the leaves, make sure that it's just about to drip off. You don't need to use more and you shouldn't add less. You should also be aware that cedar oil's smell is quite strong, and it will often linger in the bottle even long after the oil is gone.

Peppermint Oil

———

This is best at deterring slugs and spiders. For the most part, spiders should be welcome in your garden because they're crucial for a natural ecosystem. You need to resist the urge to smash spiders, and instead use the peppermint oil. Just don't spray the peppermint oil directly on the spiders or it will cause them to die. Instead, spray the oil in a zone where you don't want any spiders. Spiders smell through their feet, so they won't want to walk around surfaces that have been sprayed with peppermint. You should spray the areas that you store your planting trays, clothes, tools and gloves so that it doesn't become a spider haven.

- 50 Drops Natural Peppermint Oil
- 10 Ounces Water
- Organic Liquid Dish Soap as Needed

Just mix everything together, and shake before each use.

Easiest Vegetables to Start With

———

N ow that you're ready to start your very own Back to Eden garden, you're going to need to choose what you're going to grow. Here are some easy vegetables to start growing organically with the Back to Eden method.

Carrots

———

C arrots grow quickly at first, which makes them a perfect vegetable to start with. The root will develop quickly when it reaches the end of their growing period. Just keep it weed free, which is easy with heavy mulching. However, the seedlings do need steady moisture, so you'll need to make sure that the ground is damp even before you can put your covering back over them. Just make sur that they don't have too much moisture or the carrots will crack.

Lettuce

———

Lettuce grows almost anywhere, making it a great cool season vegetable. The ideal temperature is fifty to sixty degrees, and it doesn't do well in hot weather. It's tolerant to light freezes and frost. Keep it in the shade during the warmer season, and there are many verities that can be grown all year. However, spring and fall are the best seasons.

Chives & Green Onions

———

Gives grow great in cold weather, and it's best to plant them in early spring. Chives will take over your garden if you let it seed naturally, making them perfect for the Back to Eden method. They're also easily transplanted, so if you choose to move them to another area it won't be a problem. For this reason, a lot of people that use the Back to Eden method will grow their chives in plotted plants and transplant them to get started. Green onions and chives flourish with the mulching method.

Garlic

———

This can be splinted in spring as soon as your ground can be worked. With the Back to Eden method, your ground doesn't compact so you'll be able to plant them early. If you plant them in fall, you'll get larger bulbs that also pack a bit more flavor. You'll need to plant six to eight weeks before your first hard frost. If you're from the South, then try February or March.

Onions

Just like chives and green onions, traditional onions will also flourish with a mulching method. The best part is that they have a short growing period, and you can even get a variety that have a high tolerance to frost. Not even snow will kill them. Since onions grow best in moist soil, the mulching method does wonders.

Bell Pepper

———

Peppers are easy for many home gardeners, and they give a great burst of color to your garden. There are different varieties, but most will be fine with light frost, and they take well to damp earth.

Broccoli

This is another cold weather plant, but it's actually sensitive to heat. It'll flour but not produce an edible head if the weather is too hot. Its best during fall, but the problem you need to keep in mind is that it takes fertile soil. If you're just starting to get your ground fertile, then you'll want to hold off on this plant despite how easy it is to grow. Otherwise, you may find that your soil becomes barren.

Thyme

This is more of an herb than a vegetable, but it tends to grow in various climates. It makes fragrant ground cover, and it attracts bees to your garden, which can help other plants, especially fruit, to thrive. It's a great way to attract pollinators, and it grows great in loose soil. Just make sure that your soil doesn't become soggy either, which is why your garden placement is so vital.

Green Beans

———

G reen beans can grow in average soil, so they grow great almost anywhere in the US. With the Back to Eden method they're known to produce an even higher yield. However, keep in mind that seeds rot in cold, damp weather. They produce a crop in about two weeks, but they produce a steady crop during the summer months.

Artichokes

———

Artichokes don't do well with frost, but they are great for warmer areas. They need rich soil that's well drained, which is why they pair well with the Back to Eden method. They also need quite a bit of sun, so eight hours is ideal. If you're in a southern state, you may want to consider growing them.

Basil

———

This is another herb, but it dies at the first frost in fall. They can be grown year round indoors, but that isn't recommended with the Back to Eden method. It thrives in warmer temperature, and it needs at least six hours of sun. However, basil will usually grow back, so don't be afraid to plant it in your garden.

Tomato

———

Most people know that tomatoes are a warm weather plant that's easy to start for even new gardeners. The only thing you need to worry about is planting them near walnut trees which excrete an acid that will inhibit plant growth. Try to plant them in a sunny corner of your garden for the best results.

Potatoes

———

Potatoes are ideal for deep, loose, and well-drained soil, making them a great Back to Eden plant to start with. With the mulching method, you'll get an incredibly high yield.

Mint

———

Yet another herb that grows great, especially when mulching. The best part is that mint is a natural pest determent if you plant it around other vegetables, making it a perfect organic pest control in your Back to Eden garden. You can start it at any time so long as there is at least two months before the first fall frost. If you're planting right after winter, just wait for your soil to warm up.

Cucumber

———

Cucumbers will self-regulate how much they produce in order to maximize their yield. Just make sure to harvest the fruit as soon as it's ready. If you pick daily, under ideal conditions, they can double in size in a day. Long, warm growing seasons are best, but it will die with a light freeze or frost.

Squash & Zucchini

———

This is a warm season crop that does badly with light freezes. However, you do have winter squash that you can plant to cycle out. Harvest begins in two months for summer squash, but winter squash has a longer growing season. Though, the Back to Eden method will usually cause your squash and zucchini to grow larger. One of the biggest killers of zucchini and squash is that they're no good in dryer climates. The Back to Eden method is fantastic with producing moist earth.

Kale

———

As we covered in the FAQ section, this is a great disease and pest resistant plant that will help you to feed your chickens in the winter. If you're not sure how to use Kale, it's also a great spinach substitute. It's mostly harvested as a salad green. Kale is even known to help prevent aphid infestations.

Easiest Fruits to Grow

Y ou don't have to limit your Back to Eden garden to vegetables and herbs. You can grow fruits too, and you'll notice fruit trees in the Back to Eden film.

Strawberries

———

S trawberries are a favorite of many people, and they're versatile. They take minimal effort to grow, and you can choose from three different types. There are the June bearing ones which will give you a large crop in June. There are some that produce smaller harvests and bear throughout the year. There is also the Day neutral ones will bear a small amount throughout the season. You'll need to rejuvenate them or replace them every three to five years, but it's less of an issue with the Back to Eden method.

Blueberries

———

Berries in general are a great way to start growing fruit. Blueberries are a three season shrub that produces white flours in spring and summer fruit. They also have gorgeous foliage in fall to give your garden a little extra color. If you're having a hard time with acidic soil in your Back to Eden garden, then try planting some blueberries there. You'll need two different varieties to get the best harvest. Try a highbush blueberry, such as Bluecrop. If you are in a in a mild climate, try a southern highbush like rabbiteye.

Blackberries & Raspberries

These are always backyard favorites, and the Back to Eden method is even better. They spread everywhere, but be careful because they're covered in thorns. However, as you saw Paul prune his plants in the original Back to Eden film, these also need pruning. Luckily, it's a quick job. You'll want to choose different varieties, such as early, mid and late season ones to extend your harvest.

Grapes

———

Grape vines are easy to grow, but there is completion in harvest item. Animals and birds will try to eat the grapes before you can harvest them, so you'll need to have countermeasures in place. You'll also need to give them support, such as trellises, to grow on. Don't forget about the pruning either! It's best to pick local varieties that are best for your area.

Melons

———

If you don't want to commit to a shrub or tree, you can still grow delicious melons. One of the most common types would be cantaloupe, watermelon or honeyed, which can be grown easily in your garden with soft, fertile soil. They need moisture to grow, making them bear larger fruit due to the mulching method.

Moving On to Fruit Trees

———

P aul in the Back to Eden film grew an orchard, which goes to prove that the Back to Eden method can work perfectly to grow fruit trees if you're patient. In this chapter, we'll look at different types of fruit trees that you can grow on your own land.

Apples

———

These are one of the most popular type of fruit trees, and it's because they're easy to grow. The ideal soil pH is 6.5, but apple trees can grow well in a more acidic sol if it's well-drained and fertile. You can even get disease resistant apple trees, such as Liberty and Freedom, which are adapted to a cold hardiness that's usually found in colder zones. But there are low chill varieties like Pink Lady and Anna that go well with mid-winter climates. No matter the climate, you can chose an apple tree that will bear fruit for you and flourish in fertile soil.

Citus Trees

———

This includes satsuma, Meyer lemons, Mandarin oranges and kumquats, which are some of the easiest fruit trees to grow. They produce fragrant oils in the leaves and rind, and they have a natural protection against pests. However, they're better for warmer areas. If you live in colder climates, then it's best to stay away from citrus trees.

Pears

Unlike apples, pears are slightly less durable to the cold. However, they still grow organically in various climates. You might want to choose a variety that is resistant to fire blight such as Moonglow or Honeysweet. Asian pear trees are the worst ones that you can choose since they take routine care. You also need to be careful to harvest pears before they are fully ripe for the best results.

Cherries

———

Remember that not all cherry trees are fruit bearing, so only pick the right ones. Try a variety like Stella or Montmorency, or even North Start so that you have pie cherries. If you have a near neutral soil, then you'll easily grow these cherry trees. Dwarf cherry trees only grow twelve feet tall, but it can help to protect your crop from birds and diseases. It makes them easy to spray, ensuring a full harvest.

Nectarines & Peaches

———

Most people want these trees, but it can be hard to grow these trees organically. They require natural pest relief. They will only grow if they your soil isn't hardpan or compacted, which makes their difficulty a little easier with the Back to Eden method. There are specialized varieties that you can get to adapt to your warmer or colder climate, depending on where you live. Though, they are short lived. You will need to organically protect them from wood boring insects. You're likely going to need to replace your plants every ten years, but they may last more with Back to Eden gardening.

Plums

———

P lum trees produce fruit erratically, which means they can lose crops easily to disease or frees. These are one of the worst trees for you to pick when you're just starting out. If you're looking for the best homestead plum trees despite this, then you'll want to try sand plums in the Midwest or beach plums in the Northeast to get the best results.

More on Apple Trees

S ince apple trees are featured in the Back to Eden film, let's take a moment to look at how to grow an apple orchard all on your own if you want to put in the time and effort. Remember that with fruit trees, you need to be patient and pick the right starter for you. Of course, Paul goes on to graft different apples onto different trees, but to do this, you need to first learn to grow a regular apple tree.

Selecting the Right Variety

———

You may just go for a disease resistant apple tree variety, but that isn't enough to get started. An apple can't just be disease resistant. You need it to taste good too. Many recent introductions lack the flavor that older ones do, so you may want to stick to older varieties such as Enterprise or Liberty. There are many heirloom apples that have a good flavor as well, which makes them great for sauce pie, and even drying. Among these heirloom trees, there are tons of disease resistant ones to choose from.

Rootstock Selection & Its Importance

Rootstock is just as important as picking a disease resistant variety. You shouldn't have a tree that's taller than you can reach to start with, but you can't expect dwarf to be small enough. This can mean anything from four to sixteen feet. Dwarfing rootstocks are M27 as well as P16. These will produce a tree that's four to seven feet. Then you have Bud 491 and Bud 146, which will create a tree that's five to ten feet tall. You also have Bud 9 and M9 which creates a tree that's six to twelve feet tall. If you want a larger tree go with P2, 03 or M9 EMLA.

Just keep in mind that this isn't the only thing that will affect the size of your tree. Since your soil is more fertile with the Back to Eden gardening method, then your trees are also going to grow larger and be more fertile. If you have a smaller rootstock the sooner you'll find fruit. Usually it will only take two to three years from planting, and you'll have large fruit. Rootstock can also decide how an apple tree will adapt to climate and different soil conditions. Dwarfing rootstock are brittle, so they won't adequately anchor a tree. This is why a dwarf tree may be too small for the Back to Eden method. You'll want something in between so you don't have to stake them or regularly irrigate them.

Thinning Your Fruit

———

Y ou should thin apples that are within thirty-five to forty days of fruit set. The sooner you do it the better. Fruit size ill increase, and so will the bloom potential for next year. Once your apple blossom has become pollinated the fruit will form the seed. This will trigger the plant hormone gibberellic acid, which will promote your fruit to become larger. However, it can also inhibit the development of the flower buds for next year. So the more seeds that it produces, the fewer flowers you'll have next year.

Therefore, the next year you'd have a thinner harvest. If you thin shortly after blossoms start to fall, then this can reduce the tendency, making a healthier harvest every year. The best way to start thinning is by taking off the biggest fruit. You should leave one every six inches. In a cluster of apples, you'll find one that's slightly bigger. This is called the king blossom. If you can't see a noticeable size different then just select the one with the thickest stem.

Put in the Work Early On

———

You need to keep a healthy sapling to have a healthy adult tree. If you maintain good soil and keep the moisture levels right, then you're going to have a healthier orchard in the long run. This means you need to make sure that you have fertile soil before you plant your trees, which is easier with the Back to Eden method. You need to be aware of apple scabs, which live on the fallen leaves. Apple scabs will reproduce in winter, so you need to rake your leaves as soon as they've fallen. This doesn't mean you can't compost them! You'll also want to increase your natural protection by increasing insect predators. To do this, grow ground cover that's designed to help your trees.

Be Patient

———

You need to remember that it can take two to three years to see any fruit on your apple trees. However, if you want the best harvest in the long run, you'll want to pull all the flowers and fruit off of your trees in the first two years. This will launch your trees into production mode, and make sure that you get any apples of your trees that look like they've been infested by worms or have blemishes. It's best to try to keep six to eight inches in between your apples too, so that you can reduce disease.

Deal with Imperfection

———

Remember that natural fruit is never going to be perfect, especially if you're going for flavor over looks. It's okay to have apples with a few scars on the outside. They can still be used for a sauce or pie.

Pruning Fruit Trees

In the Back to Eden film, it shows Paul pruning his fruit tree so they provide a better harvest. Yet, pruning trees can seem like a lot of work and most people don't know where to start.

Cutting to the Line

———

There are many different teaching methods about pruning trees, but all of them will tell you that you don't cut the collar. This is the line of a tree where a new branch is starting. If you cut beyond it, then you leave a stump which will grow suckers. It makes the tree ugly, and it'll eventually rot the tree and cause it to create a cavity. Paul tells you that the line is there for a reason, so he cuts right to the line, and the trees healed wonderfully in the film.

Quality Tools

———

Pruning loppers are bad for your garden, and Paul doesn't recommend them. They keep you from getting close enough to the line, and on top of that they crush the wood. They don't provide a clean cut. You want a nice clean cut for the best results, and in the film Paul recommends two trees. The Felo F-8 Classic Pruner with Comfortable Ergonomic Design is one of them. It has a strong anvil blade, making it great for day to day pruning. You can cut back overgrown hydrangea or you can remove a sickly pansy patch with minimal stress. This tool won't help with your wrist or hand. They're crafted with Swiss carbon steel blades, and that makes them resist rust with frictionless slicing too. They can cut through stems, wires and branch up to an inch in diameter.

You may also want to try the Samurai Ichiban 330Mm Pruning Saw Scabbard. This tool has a thirteen inch pruning saw, and it allows for precise and smooth cutting. They taper ground and thinner, so they cut easily and quickly. They have permanently filed teeth, and they're certainly a durable tool. They're even covered for comfort, as well as being nonslip. You can buy a replacement blade if necessary too. They have two common blade profiles which are non-tapered and tapered. If you use a style tooth, then it'll cut faster than the two sided tooth which is conventional. If a blade has a higher number of teeth per inch, then it's a fine tooth blade.

Remember It's Art

Remember that it's art and not just a science. Never cut more than a third of your tree because it'll send your tree into panic mode. It'll send up root suckers, which will be counterproductive to its growth. You want to open the tree to sunlight, removing damaged or even diseased limbs, and stimulate growth in your trees. So take your pruning carefully, and don't be afraid to learn as you go.

As far as learning to open it up to sun, you'll want to make it where the Am or morning sun can get in. moistures on your branches and leaves will lead to disease and mold, which can easily kill off your fruit trees. Your fruit will also ripen in the sun, so that's another great reason to open up your trees. Damaged and diseased limbs will just suck out the life from your tree. You don't want your tree trying to waste energy recovering when it can be supporting new growth instead. Your tree will try to go to sleep when it's winter, but by pruning it, the sap flows through the tree again. This will keep it stimulated so that it can grow year round.

Shape Your Tree

———

You'll also want to shape your tree, and this isn't because it's an art form. When you shape your tree, you make it easier for your tree to bear fruit where it's easy to access or for the sun to hit it properly. Your tree should have different levels, and if your levels cross each over, then they won't grow as well. Fruit won't want to grow on vertical branches and vertical branches will cross over others, so it's best to get rid of vertical branches before they grow too much.

You'll then want to narrow down which horizontal branches to cut. If three limbs are coming close together, then you'll want to take the middle out. This will give more space to the other two. If a branch curves back into the tree, then it's a branch that should be taken out as well. If a branch gets too low to the ground, then cut it back so that your fruit doesn't spoil.

Organic Fertilizer

———

I f you don't plan to raise chickens, you may need to use some organic
fertilizer from time to time in your Back to Eden garden. It'll speed
the process along so that your soil gets where you need it to be, and it'll
help it to stay that way for a long time to come.

Worm Casting

———

This is a soil superfood, and it'll provide nitrogen which will help to make your soil more absorbent. It's full of beneficial bacteria and microbes.

Tea

———

Tea bags don't just taste great and calm your nerves, they're perfect for your garden too. The tea bags as they decompose will release nitrogen. You need to first make sure you're buying tea bags that are able to decompose naturally. Otherwise you may end up with ones that are made from polypropylene. If the bag is slippery, you probably shouldn't use it in your garden. You can also brew tea for acid loving plants such as blueberries or azaleas. It'll also help to deter root maggots!

Beer

This one is still debated. There are people that think beer doesn't do anything, but other people believe that they don't do anything at all. It's a simple sugar, but your plants need a complex sugar. However, even if it doesn't work to fertilize your garden, it will help to get rid of slugs. If you brew your own beer, you can even use beer mash, which are grains leftover from the beer making, which will help to fertilize your soil.

Bone Meal

———

You're likely to not have this lying around the house, but it's a great source of protein and phosphorus. It's coarsely ground waste products and animal bones. Just check your soil to make sure you need phosphorus before you ad it. You'll want to use as soil test to do so. If you want to make your own bone meal, you'll just need to store bones in your freezer and clean them by making a bone broth. Once they're sterilized, then bake them under a broiler for teen to fifteen minutes, and then dry them. Let them dry on the counter for three to four weeks, and then you can crush them into a fine powder. Some people use a food processor too, but other people prefer a mortar and pestle. Just wear a mask over your nose and mouth.

Coconut Coir

―――

Coconut coir can replace Peat moss, which is non-renewable. It adds air and space, making it a great addition to mulching methods. It'll help with water retention and it'll help with nutrient uptake. It can help you to start seedlings easier too.

Newspaper

———

You already know that you'll need to add either cardboard or newspaper, but here's another reason to use newspaper instead. Soy based ink kills various diseases in soil. It may be easier if you shred it first or apply it wet. Do not use glossy inserts since the colored inks and finishes on your newspaper can be toxic to your plants.

Urine

⸻

This grosses many people out, but it's a great source of nitrogen. You can add it to your compost pile or your compost tea, which will help to activate the process. Within twenty four hours of leaving your body the disease, toxins and pathogens are killed, so there's no need to worry. Just start by diluting the water in a 1:2 ration to water your plants.

Seaweed or Kelp Meal

Kelp contains small amounts of phosphorous, potassium and nitrogen, but it has a high count of trace elements that can help your garden too. You'd want to mix this with water, and you can use it as a foliar spray or pour it onto the soil around your plants for the best results.

Citus Rinds

―――

You may not have a lot of these lying around, but there's no reason to waste anything, especially if you're growing fruit trees. Just place them right under your covering, and that's all you need. They'll release calcium, potassium, sulfur, magnesium and other nutrients as they break down. You can dry the peels and grind them to a fine powder to add to your soil too, but applying them directly is just easier.

Granite Dust

You'll likely have to buy this organic fertilizer, but it's usually made from volcanic rock. It has over sixty elements, including magnesium calcium, potassium and phosphorus to help your soil. Your soil will be nutrient dense in no time, but always read the label.

White Vinegar

———

I f you need to change the pH level of your soil, then white vinegar can help. It's still debated if it's temporary or not. This is a great organic fertilizer if you're using the Back to Eden method in container gardens. Just feed your plants a mixture with a tablespoon of sugar, a cup of water and a tablespoon of vinegar. Mix it well, and shake before using. The sugar should be completely dissolved before you use it, and you'll want to apply it below your covering.

Mushrooms

———

Mushrooms aren't just good for eating, they're good for your soil too. The mushroom that you can see is the fruiting body. The magic happens in the soil, and they a part of a soil web that will bring nutrients to the plants you're growing.

Chicken Feathers

———

I f you're already raising chickens to use their eggs and manure, then you'll want to use the loose fathers too. If you're raising chickens for meat, then this is another great way not to waste any part of the animal. Chicken feathers add nitrogen to your compost pile, but you won't want to put them directly into your garden yet. Let them decompose first.

Rabbit Droppings

―――

M any people own a rabbit for a pet or raise them for meat, and you can actually collect rabbit droppings in your area too. If there is a rabbit meat farm near you, contact them and see if you can take some of the droppings off of their hands. You can add it directly to your soil or your compost pile.

Shellfish

If you leave shellfish, then you don't want to throw the shells either. The bacteria that breaks them down is important, so simmer your shells in boiling water for twenty to thirty minutes. Drain well, and then place them in a food dehydrator until they're dry enough to crush. Add it to your compost pile or directly to your soil for the best results.

Baking Soda

———

B aking soda will help to discourage pests and they'll sweeten tomatoes too. Lightly sprinkle it over your soil for the best results.

Nut Shells

———

Nut shells need to be tossed aside, but that doesn't mean that you need to throw them in the trash. Nut shells will add bulk, and it'll help to fluff up your covering. Microbes are great for your garden, and your nut shells will provide them.

Organic Composting

———

C omposting isn't hard, so here is yet another way to make wonderful organic fertilizer for your Back to Eden garden.

Set Up Some Space

———

No matter what you do, food will rot. All you have to do is help it along to compost properly. You can fence in an area in your yard if you have moderate temperatures. Usually a three by three by three space is ideal for a small garden, but if you're making a larger one you may want make a bigger compost area. Place your scrap pile on the ground, and you'll have no issue getting it started. Though, if you want to be tidier then you can buy bins. There are even drums that tumble which will aerate your compost and help to convert it to compost quicker. Even if you're using the Back to Eden method in your apartment, you can get indoor bins to make your own compost. Just stock them with critter sand worms that you get online.

Mixing Properly

———

If you do composting right, you won't notice it's there. You need to create a proper balance of materials which will help to break everything down with minimal or no odor. You'll want to add two to three parts browns, which will be carbon heavy to every one part nitrogen centric compost material, which is green. The browns can include paper, dead leaves, food-soiled paper napkins or other paper. For your greens toss in vegetable bits and fruit. Breads can also go in there as well as filters, coffee grounds and grass clippings, which will all be greens. If you don't want to always run out to toss everything in your yard, then designate a pale under your sink or table. Some people prefer to use a bag in the freezer too, but it's completely up to you.

Be Selective

You don't have to compost everything if it isn't going to compost well. There are still some food scraps that you need simply toss in the trash. You'll want to get rid of bones, dairy products or meat. Your compost many not reach the right temperatures to kill pathogens that might be in these items. They will also lure pests to your compost. You don't want to deal with skunks or cats in your compost. For the same reason you need to stay away from olive oil and other oils.

What You Can Compost

———

Here is a basic rundown of what you can compost easily!

- Fruits & Vegetables
- Uncoated Cardboard, Ripped Small
- Eggshells
- Fireplace Ashes, Only from natural Wood
- Glass Clippings
- Fur & Hair
- Straw & Hay
- Houseplants
- Newspaper, Shredded
- Leaves
- Paper, Uncoated & in Small Pieces
- Nutshells
- Tea Bags
- Wood Chips
- Sawdust
- Yard Trimmings

What You Can't compost

———

H ere are some things you should avoid adding into your compost.

- Twigs or Tree Leaves form Black Walnuts
- Charcoal Ash or Coals
- Dairy Products & Eggs
- Insect Ridden Plants
- Diseased Plants
- Fats, Grease, Lard & Oils
- Meat or Fish Scraps & Bones
- Pet Litter or Feces
- Yard trimming that has Pesticides or has been treated with chemicals.

Let it Rot

———

There's little to no maintenance with your compost pile. You just need to let the rot set in. turn your pile once a week with a shovel or old garden fork in the summer. In the winter, you only need to do so once every three to four weeks. You'll also want to sprinkle soil from your garden onto each layer which will help to put in beneficial organisms. A little water can go a long ways too. Grab a handful of your pile to see if it needs water. It should feel as damp as a wrung out cloth or sponge.

Use it Wisely

Your compost is ready when your soil is dark and you can't recognize anything you dropped in. spread it around your plants as needed. You should prioritize where you put the fertilizer based on where you fertilized last time so that you can cycle your compost in different areas of your garden.

Worm Composting

———

You already know that worms do wonders for your organic compost pile, and they're easy to get. You don't even need to buy them if you don't want to!

Acquiring Your Worms

———

It doesn't matter if you're trying to buy your worms or collect them yourself, then all you need to do is follow the tips below.

Check Online

There are many blogs out there that discuss compost worms. Many of them will sell compost worms as well, but you need to be discerning. Some sites are obviously better than others. You might want to check usually buy a pound for under twenty-five dollars.

Check Bait & Tackle Shops

———

Worms are commonly used for fishing, so checking your local bait and tackle shops is always a good idea. You can usually pay under four dollars for thirty-five worms, and they sell them year round. The best part is that you have no need to wait to get them in the mail! However, you don't want to purchase a full pound of worms per pound. Since a pound is roughly 60-100 worms, then it'll cost over sixty dollars at a bait and tackle show. Though, you can start with about sixty to seventy worms, and that will usually be enough.

Check Your Farmer's Market

—————

If you want to avoid shipping costs, then a local farmers market might be the right place too. However, not every farmers market will carry worms.

Internet Search

———

You can usually do a quick search for free worms, and there are sometimes people giving them away if they have too many in their compost. However, this can be a bit of a longshot.

Collect Them Yourself

You'll want to collect them yourself if you really want to save money, and if you have a big property this won't be hard at all!

Collecting Worms Yourself

I f you really want to get worms for free, then you're going to want to collect them yourself. Remember that it's sometimes easier to just have your compost pile on the ground so that this isn't necessarily. Sadly, that isn't an option for everyone so here are a few ways to collect compost worms.

The Rainstorm Method

———

For this method you'll need to go out in the rainstorm or right after it. It's going to be dark, so you'll need a flashlight. It's easier to locate night crawlers since they'll be roaming around because of the wet conditions. Remember that worms have to stay moist to survive. Use a shovel to dig into your ground, and then look for the worms by hand.

Just Dig

———

J ust dig for worms where they're likely to be such as near a perennial sterm, especially if there are fallen leaves. They can be found near mud or bodies of water too. Check underneath things that are damp too such as logs, rocks or even rotten things. Worms can sense vibrations though, so you'll want to be stealthy and look quickly.

Cardboard Boxes

———

This is one of the easiest methods to gathering your worms, and all you need to do is leave a wet piece of cardboard in the yard overnight. Make sure it's flattened first though. This will attract your worms to the surface, and then when you remove your cardboard, you can just collect the worms underneath. It's best to do this before the ground heats up, so get up early in the morning.

Worm Composting FAQ

———

Here are some FAQ that you can use to get started.

Do I need to use worms in a compost pile?

―――――

It can help to speed the process up, but you really don't need to add worms to outside composting. You need to do this in the bin. Worms will often find their way into a compost pile all on their own.

Do I need a compost activator?

———

You don't really need to spend the money. Commercially sold compost bio activators contain microorganisms, but these can be found in soil too. Just add soil instead.

Aren't the worms in the worm bin the same as earthworms?

———

The biggest issue with this type of thinking is that when people think of earthworms they think night crawlers. These can be eight to ten inches long and a half inch in diameter. Night crawlers are not h same as red wigglers, but both can be called earthworms. Night crawlers are soil dwellers, so they'll burrow a few feet below the surface. This mixes different layers of soil, aerating it. Red wigglers are surface dwellers, so they are in the top six inches of your soil. Red wigglers are better for your compost pile.

Do I have to worry about worms biting me?

———

No, you don't have to worry about your worms biting you because worms don't bite.

What is the yellow liquid that my worms release?

———

M any people guess that this is urine, but it's not the case. It's a caulomic fluid, and a worm will release it when it's stressed. They do this to keep their body moist, so if you pick it up, that's likely what's going to happen.

Why is worm compost so helpful?

———

It easily makes nutrients available to plants. The worms change the nutrients from your food into a form that your plants can process.

Troubleshooting

———

Here are some common problems you may be having with your worm composting, and some easy solutions.

There are unpleasant and strong odors in your compost pile or bin.

———

This is because your food is rotting, and your worms aren't able to eat it all. This is what causes the smell. The solution is so to stop adding food waste until your worms have broken down what they have so, you may want to freeze the waste or add more worms to your compost. Also make sure you aren't adding meat or greasy foods which cause odor problems. You can also stir the contents of your pile to give it more air, which will reduce the odors. You need to check to see if your bin has drainage holes if you aren't putting your compost directly on the ground too. Your worms can drown if the bin is too wet.

There are fruit flies around my compost.

———

If you bury your food, you shouldn't have a problem with fruit flies in the first place. Also, this can all lead back to your worms being overloaded too. If you're still having issues, keep a plastic sheet on the surface of your bin or pile. If your flies persist, then move your compost to a different area. A few friendly spiders around your bin can help too.

Worms are crawling out of my compost pile!

———

This could be because your bedding is too acidic, which will make your worms migrate. This can happen if you've added too many acidic foods such as citrus peels. Just reduce the amount of acidic matter you're adding into your bin for a while.

Some Final Tips

———

Remember that the Back to Eden gardening method is just a type of organic gardening that encourages you to stay true to God's designs. You're meant to be patient, but it can be hard if you're just getting started. Here are some final organic gardening tips to help you out.

Easy Seed Starting

You may be tempted to head to your local home and garden store and start by buying some expensive seed starters, but this isn't necessary with the Back to Eden method. You can up-cycle everyday items like eggshells, newspaper, and citrus peels to give your seedlings a copy place to sprout. No need to spend more money then you have to! If you're a coffee fiend, consider starting your seeds in your empty K-cup containers too.

Support Plants

You should never be afraid to support plants that need it. Even in the Back to Eden film, you'll see Paul supporting some plants briefly that need it. For example, he has to support his apple trees when they first got started because their fruit was too heavy for their limbs. There is nothing wrong with giving your plants a little extra help along the way.

Recycle Your Eggshells

This is even more important if you plan to raise ducks or chickens. Everything was designed with a purpose in mind by the Creator, so there's no reason you can't recycle your eggs to help your garden along. You can keep them in one area and sprinkle them after they dry out and are crushed or just throw them in the compost pile.

Cover Your Compost

———

If your compost has finished and you can't use it for a while, then place a tarp over it so that the sun doesn't leach the nutrients out of it. There's no reason to let all of your hard work go to waste!

Don't Rush

———

P aul's garden wasn't built in a day. It took him over a decade to get the garden that he wanted. You have to be patient with your soil, your plants, and you have to accept that there will be times when things don't go the way that you want them to. This is all part of the learning process. Many people get mixed results with the Back to Eden method because they try to rush through it. However, if you're patient and take your time, don't let failure stop you, you'll soon have a garden that you can be proud of and will take much less labor and time. There's no reason that you can't be self-sufficient and grow enough fruits and vegetables for you, your family or even to sell if you choose to!

Don't Use Railroad Ties

———

When you're working with a Back to Eden garden, upcycling may sound appealing. Still, railroad ties aren't something you need to use. They can leach chemicals into your garden, and they can be both harmful and toxic.

Pinch off Flowers

———

I f you pinch off flowers frequently then you are setting your plants into overdrive. It's the same reason you prune your apple trees for the first few years by pinching off the apples before they grow.

Welcome Bats

───

You don't want to chase bats away from your garden! Bats are a natural form of pest control, and their droppings are great for your garden too. Many North American bats feed exclusively on pests, which will help to control your bug population.

Begin with the Soil

———

Don't rush getting your soil perfect. You need to take your time and not cut corners. Your garden will begin or end with your soil. Pest management begins with soil too. Your soil will provide nutrients to your food. Your soil will produce healthy plants. Your soil will help fight of diseases. Your soil is the most important part of your garden.

Reuse Water

If you feel like you need to water a particular section of your garden while you get your soil properly developed, try reusing water. You can ruse water from cooking or washing vegetables. You can also collect rainwater or even dilute your urine.

Use Sticks

I f you're having a hard time keeping birds from destroying your seedlings then put sticks upright around them. It'll keep birds from destroying your garden, and it'll keep cats from laying on your seedlings too.

Soak Your Seeds

———

You may want to try to soak your seeds in warm water the day before you plant them too. This can make a huge difference in how well they take off, and it will help to minimize the work involved.

Pre-Sprout Seeds

———

If you don't have a green thumb when trying to grow seeds in the dirt, try germinating them before you put them in the ground. All you need is a wet paper towel. Place your seed in the middle of it, and then fold your paper towel around it. Make sure that it stays moist, and then just give it a few days.

Don't be Afraid to Plan

———

You should never be afraid to plan your garden out. Your garden is what you're going to be putting a lot of time into, so think about what you want to do with it. Research what plants will grow best in the acidify you already have in your soil. Research what plants will grow best in the amount of sunlight and rainfall you get year round. Research what plants will grow best if you don't have a lot of time, and research what plants will grow best in the climate that you have naturally. All of this research will pay off in the long run.

Sign Up for Free News, Tips and Tricks and more at:

http://www.FunHappyLives.com

Conclusion

Now you know everything you need to know about the Back to Eden gardening method, you can start working on your own little slice of Eden. With the tips and tricks in this book, you can expand on what the Back to Eden film taught you so that you can create a fruitful garden that meets all of your needs and desires. It doesn't matter if you're growing fruits or vegetables. You can start your composting process and grow nutritious, healthy foods that will sure to sustain you and your family! Remember to be patient and stick to organic, all natural methods to have a fruitful and full garden that's ready in no time at all.

One more thing, if you enjoyed this book, please leave a review at the retailer's site where you purchased your copy. It will be greatly appreciated.

Don't miss out!

Visit the website below and you can sign up to receive emails whenever Bo Tucker publishes a new book. There's no charge and no obligation.

https://books2read.com/r/B-A-ETXF-RATS

Connecting independent readers to independent writers.